BEGINNING GROUND WORK

Everything We've Learned About
Relationship and Leadership

Copyright © 2011 by Joe Camp

Photos © 2011 by Kathleen Camp

Published in the United States by 14 Hands Press,

an imprint of Camp Horse Camp, LLC

www.14handspress.com

Some of the material herein has appeared

in other books by Joe Camp

Library of Congress subject headings

Camp, Joe

Beginning Ground Work / by Joe Camp

Horses

Human-animal relationships

Horses-training

Horsemanship

The Soul of a Horse: Life Lessons from the Herd

ISBN 978-1-930681-42-2

First Edition

BEGINNING GROUND WORK

*Everything We've Learned About
Relationship and Leadership*

JOE CAMP

14 HANDS PRESS

Also by Joe Camp

The National Best Seller
The Soul of a Horse
Life Lessons from the Herd

The Highly Acclaimed Best Selling Sequel
Born Wild
The Soul of a Horse

Amazon # 1
Horses & Stress
Eliminating the Root Cause of Most Health, Hoof & Behavior Problems

Amazon # 1
Why Relationship First Works
Why and How It Changes Everything

Training with Treats
*With Relationship and Basic Training Locked In
Treats Can Be an Excellent Way to Enhance Good Communication*

Why Our Horses Are Barefoot
Everything We've Learned About the Health and Happiness of the Hoof

God Only Knows
Can You Trust Him with the Secret?

The Soul of a Horse Blogged
The Journey Continues

Horses Were Born To Be On Grass
*How We Discovered the Simple But Undeniable
Truth About Grass, Sugar, Equine Diet & Lifestyle*

Horses Without Grass
*How We Kept Six Horses Moving and Eating Happily
Healthily on an Acre and a Half of Rocks and Dirt*

Who Needs Hollywood
The Amazing Story of How Benji Became the #3 Movie of the Year

Dog On It
Everything You Need To Know About Life Is Right There At Your Feet

"Joe Camp is a master storyteller." - *THE NEW YORK TIMES*

"Joe Camp is a natural when it comes to understanding how animals tick and a genius at telling us their story. His books are must-reads for those who love animals of any species." - *MONTY ROBERTS, AUTHOR OF NEW YORK TIMES BEST-SELLER THE MAN WHO LISTENS TO HORSES*

"Camp has become something of a master at telling us what can be learned from animals, in this case specifically horses, without making us realize we have been educated, and, that is, perhaps, the mark of a real teacher. The tightly written, simply designed, and powerfully drawn chapters often read like short stories that flow from the heart." - *JACK L. KENNEDY, THE JOPLIN INDEPENDENT*

"One cannot help but be touched by Camp's love and sympathy for animals and by his eloquence on the subject." - *MICHAEL KORDA, THE WASHINGTON POST*

"Joe Camp is a gifted storyteller and the results are magical. Joe entertains, educates and empowers, baring his own soul while articulating keystone principles of a modern revolution in horsemanship." - *RICK LAMB, AUTHOR AND TV/RADIO HOST "THE HORSE SHOW"*

For Kathleen, who loved me enough to initiate all this
when she was secretly terrified of horses

CONTENTS

INTRODUCTION

Often, in the early evening, when the stresses of the day are weighing heavy, I pack it in and head out to the pasture. I'll sit on my favorite rock, or just stand, with my shoulders slumped, head down, and wait. It's never long before I feel the magical tickle of whiskers against my neck, or the elixir of warm breath across my ear, a restoring rub against my cheek. I have spoken their language and they have responded. And my problems have vanished. This book is written for everyone who has never experienced this miracle.

- Joe Camp
The Soul of a Horse
Life Lessons from the Herd

PREREQUISITE

I remember well the day our first three horses arrived. Such a rush! The result of a 66-year love affair... from afar. In my mind, and heart. And suddenly there were three horses in our family. It felt magical.

Now what?

The urge to climb on and hit the trails was compelling. We have horses. Let's ride. Let's go. Let's do *some*thing.

Fortunately for all concerned we had a better plan. Thanks to a chance reading of an article by Monty Roberts we were going to begin at the beginning with relationship first.

Before riding.

Before training.

Before anything.

And ultimately we discovered that it was the single most important thing we could've done.

Many trainers and clinicians begin with step number two. Leadership. Obviously a very important step. But it's step number two. Because when you get the relationship right first, everything changes. Absolutely everything. Your horse now cares about his time with you. He is more giving, more willing. And he tries harder.

Stacy Westfall says that the best thing she's ever done for her training is to get the relationship right before she does any training.

Which is why my eBook Nugget *Why Relationship First Works* is a prerequisite to this book, or to any book or DVD on training and leadership. Or read the original *The Soul of a Horse – Life Lessons from the Herd*. But please-please-please read one of them and get your relationship right with your horse *before* you begin groundwork.

You will never be sorry you did.

- Joe Camp

1

LEADERSHIP

I am not a trainer. I'm a lover of horses. I don't train horses other than our own. And I really don't train people. I just introduce them to the needs of the horse, the whys, the ways to communicate, and what can be accomplished with some mileage.

Pat Parelli says that sending your horse out to a trainer is like sending your spouse out to a trainer. If you love your horse why would you want him to have this amazing relationship with some stranger? You want that relationship to be with you, right?

Kathleen's and my journey with horses has been relatively short by most standards. But full of astounding discoveries by any standard. We began with a clean plate. Rank novices. Five years ago we had no horses and no clue. And today we can proudly point to two books chronicling our journey that are changing the lives of horses for the better all across the planet.

We've learned that most of the issues and problems that owners have with their horses stem from the fact that they did not begin at the beginning. With Relationship First. And only then move on to Leadership. Some call it *respect*. But basically, it's ground work.

You learn in *Why Relationship First Works* that when your horse accepts you, of his own free choice, to be a member of his herd, once he says to you *I trust you to be my leader* then everything changes. He becomes more willing, more giving. And he tries harder.

But... along with all that he's looking for good leadership, and if he doesn't get it he will take back his trust and become *your* leader. That's the way it is in the herd. *Who moves who* is the way the pecking order in any herd sorts itself out. So before you can become the leader your horse is looking for, you must first understand his language and how that language works in the herd, even if it's only a herd of two.

That's what ground work is all about. Who moves who? But from our experience I can tell you that it's *very* helpful to spend some time out with the herd, soaking up the way they interact and what each little nuance means and accomplishes. If you don't have a herd handy buy or borrow Ginger Kathrens' excellent PBS series of three specials about the wild stallion Cloud and his herd. Only after you've proven to the horse that you understand *his* language, should you begin to expand his horizons by asking him to understand yours.

Without ever touching Cash, completely at liberty, he will disengage his hindquarters and move his butt left or right with just a look or a point from me. He'll do the same with his forequarters. With a mere request he will walk forward, or back up, or walk with me at my shoulder, flex left or right touching his nose to his side and holding that position until I say "okay". He smiles, he bows, he side passes with just a point, he kisses, and he waves hello with either front foot. Again, all at liberty. No lead rope.

It didn't start out that way I promise you.

Our growing library of books and DVDs all said begin at the beginning. But for them the beginning meant standing in the arena teaching my horse to back up, or move sideways. Or come to me. These exercises would give me control, said the DVDs. And once I had complete control over how, where, and when the horse moves, I would then have a safe horse.

But I wanted to know why.

I was also anxious to take the next step with Cash. After Join-Up, he was now looking to me for leadership, so off we went to the arena.

I hear we learn by our mistakes.

One of the training DVDs had spelled out three different ways to teach backup.

See Cash back up, Method One.

See Cash back up, Method Two.

See Cash back up, Method Three.

Why, I wondered, did I need three? Especially here, beginning at the beginning. One method would've been quite enough to confuse both of us this first time out.

See Joe look like a circus clown.

Clumsy and awkward do not adequately describe the moment. I had Cash's lead rope in one hand and a three-foot-long Handy Stick in the other. A Handy Stick is a plastic rod used to extend the length of one's arm so that, hopefully, one can stand back far enough to avoid an accidental knockdown like Kathleen got to experience (but that's another story). The stick, sold of course by one of the DVD trainers, is not to be used for discipline, only for guidance. According to this particular DVD, I was supposed to be doing one thing with the lead rope and another with the stick.

It was like trying to rub circles on your belly with one hand while patting your head with the other.

I felt like an idiot.

Those droll cocks of the head and quizzical looks from Cash were coming at me like machine-gun fire. I expected him to burst out laughing any minute. I was clearly not getting through. But something else was bothering me, something beyond beginner's clumsiness. Cash and I had bonded just a few days before in the round pen, and this exercise was not strengthening that bond.

I was trying to learn a specific task, or, rather, trying to *teach* a specific task.

Or both, I suppose.

But what I wanted most was to understand what made this huge wonderful beast tick, how he learns, how I could communicate clearly with him, what it meant to him when I did this with the rope or that with the stick. Only then could I better figure out how to get Cash to understand what he clearly wasn't understanding on this particular day. I was trying to follow a DVD's instruction, move by move, when what I felt I should've been doing was experiencing this from his end of the rope.

It wasn't long before Cash sent me straightaway back to the books and DVDs, which, I soon discovered, had no intention of teaching me how to understand Cash until I first knew how to back him up. And move him sideways. And so on.

Truth be told, I actually went back to determine whether the stick was supposed to be in the right or left hand. As if it made a difference to Cash.

But I found myself skipping ahead, to the end of the series. Looking for some conceptual meat. Then to the end of the next series. Racing past the task-based learning. Searching for comprehension, meaning. Something that would connect the dots. What I found is that all these programs pretty much never get there until the end.

How backward, I thought.

Now that you've come this far, we're going to teach you why all these tasks we've taught you work. We're going to show you how to understand the horse so you can figure things out for yourself.

But I didn't want to wait. Not that the tasks don't have good and proper purpose. It's just that they would mean so much more to both of us, to me and the horse, if I understood why he was getting it, and why he wanted to. Learning, then, would surely happen so much faster. His *and* mine.

The early lessons in the books and DVDs never said, *Before you start this program go spend a few days out in the pasture just watching the interaction of the herd. Making note of how the smallest of gestures, when delivered accurately, can get the desired result.*

Wow! Why wasn't that up front?

I went immediately to the pasture. And watched.

Again and again.

The DVDs didn't explain, in the early lessons, that when a leader horse swells up and pins her ears and moves toward a follower's butt, it means move that butt. Now! And that such a move doesn't mean *I don't like you.* Or *I want you out of my pasture.* It simply means, *I am the leader here and I want you to move your butt over.* That's it. A few minutes later the same two horses will be huddled next to each other, head to tail, swishing flies out of each other's faces.

This is a difficult concept for humans to grasp. We are such emotional beings. We don't like to hurt another's feelings. Usually. So it's hard for us to realize that, with horses, such behavior is simply leadership in action. And is actually building respect for the leader.

It was important for me to learn that the horse was not going to think less of me if I swelled up like a predator, pinned my ears, and pointed at his hindquarters. He would actually think more. *Hey, this guy knows the language. Cool. I respect that.*

And then it struck me: These horses accepted me in Join-Up. I'm *supposed* to be part of the herd. It stands to reason that I need to know how to behave like a herd leader.

The hard part was remembering to swell up. And I had trouble pinning my ears. I suppose that's why we have fingers. And eyebrows. Eyebrows are good.

I was beginning to understand that, in effect, we must find a way to be a horse. We shouldn't even try to relate horse behavior and communication to human equivalents. Or even doggie equivalents. Horses are not humans. And they aren't dogs. If you treat a horse like a puppy, you will never be his leader. I'm not saying you shouldn't give your horse a hug or a rub. But a dog will do virtually anything for a hug. A horse will do virtually nothing for a hug. But he will do virtually anything for his respected leader. And he will continually test that leader to see if he or she is still worthy of the title.

It was in the pasture that I learned all this, and began to understand how to be a horse. I had finally found where I was to begin. I was ecstatic.

None of the DVDs had said any of this early enough to suit me. And very few effectively embraced the concept of how a horse learns until well down in the program. Simply understanding what *reward* is to a horse made so much difference in the way I approached the task of training. But like learning to get out into the pasture, I had to skip ahead in those DVDs to find it.

Reward for a horse, I finally discovered, true reward, comes from release of pressure.

And with that reward comes learning. Communication. Understanding.

It's as simple as that.

In the wild, when being chased by a cougar, the horse's reward is when the cougar turns back.

Release of the pressure.

And so it is in the herd. When the matriarch disciplines the foal by sending him away from the herd, and pressures him to stay away, it is the release of that pressure, when the foal submits, that is his reward. As the foal begins to understand what it takes to avoid the pressure, he will submit earlier the next time. And, hopefully, not be a bad boy at all the third time.

When a dominant leader says, *Move your butt over,* the instant the follower responds, the leader drops the pressure. The lesson: *If I move my butt when she applies pressure, she will release the pressure and I will no longer feel uncomfortable.*

The next time that same horse will move his butt sooner. And before long, a simple look from the leader will do the job. No swelling up. No pointed movements. Maybe just a drop of the ears. Or a flick of the head.

And so it is as we teach. It's not so much what we do, but rather the release of pressure the very instant the horse gives even a hint of the desired response. "Reward the slightest try." Clinton Anderson says. Then, depending upon the horse, it usually doesn't take long to reach the conclusion: *Oh, I get it. If I move over when Joe does that he releases the pressure so that must be what he wants.*

In effect this is an extension of the doctrine of choice. *Do I want the pressure or the comfort of no pressure. I think I'll move over and thereby choose no pressure.*

Maybe Kathleen and I are weird, but we agree that having a thorough understanding of how a horse learns, and how the herd teaches one another, how they receive information and understanding, would provide so much more insight into the training process. And be a richer foundation from which to launch.

Concept-based learning.

This all came together for me one day as I was scanning a DVD and stumbled onto a very simple little exercise with an in-depth conceptual analysis of why it worked. The exercise was simply to get the horse to lower his head when asked. No sticks involved. No arenas. No stumbling around trying to rub my belly while patting my head. Just me and Cash. Up close and personal.

The lesson began with understanding that all horses, by nature, resist pressure. And lean into pressure. When you push on his shoulder he'll lean into you. Pull down on an unschooled horse's halter and he will resist and pull up. That's because the pressure, to him, is actually at the top of the halter. He feels the top strap pushing down. So he pushes into that pressure by lifting his head. These are genetic traits, embedded for survival. When a wolf sinks his teeth into a horse's underbelly, the horse's only chance for survival is to push down, to apply pressure to the wolf. If the horse pulls away from the wolf he helps the predator rip his belly open.

So how do you get the horse to understand that you want his head to go down? How do you communicate that when he wants to push against the pressure by raising his head?

How would I do it with a dog? How would I get Benji to understand a desired action?

I would reward him with a treat.

And what is reward to a horse, at least for now? I asked myself with a knowing smile.

Release of pressure. Comfort, I said smugly.

And off I went to gather Monsieur le Cash.

This time it went swimmingly. I applied the slightest of downward pressure to the lead rope. Not trying to pull his head down. Just enough to counter his upward resistance. And I held it. The discomfort to Cash was minimal. Just the pressure of the rope halter. Before long, Cash lowered his head, just enough to release the pressure, and I immediately dropped the lead rope, rubbed him on the forehead, and praised him.

Then we did it again. This time he dropped his head sooner, and went further down, and I released the rope, as Clinton Anderson says, like it was a hot potato.

Before long, Cash's response was almost instantaneous, dropping his head as much as ten to twelve inches. I pulled out a folding chair and sat down to see if he would drop all the way to my lap. Three sets of pressure and release, and he was there. I could've bridled him from the chair. Granted, Cash is very intuitive. He gets things quickly and is very willing. Others of our horses would take longer. But now they all have learned this task.

What about treats, some might ask. Wouldn't he learn all this even more quickly if he were getting a treat instead of just a release of pressure? Something he actually likes? As mentioned above, only after you've proven to the horse that you understand *his* language, should you begin to expand his horizons by asking him to understand yours. It's very important that, in the beginning, you stick to learning and communicating in his language. Once done, have a look at our eBook Nugget *Training with Treats*.

The next step was to ask Cash to leave his head down, rather than immediately lift it up upon the release of pressure. To communicate that, when I released the rope, I released it just a little. When he lifted up, he bumped back into pressure from the rope, and immediately dropped again.

He was soon staying down until I completely released the rope and said, "Okay. Good boy."

I was grinning from ear to ear.

Not so much because he had done the task, but because I had watched his wheels turn. I had seen the intake of understanding that I was asking for something that was completely counter to his genetics, but because I was a trusted leader he could respond safely, without worry. Willingly.

And he did.

We tromped up the driveway to the front door of our house and I called for Kathleen.

"Come out! I've gotta show you something!" You would've thought I had found the cure for cancer.

The door swung open and she almost swallowed the plum she was eating. She had never seen a horse at the front door before. Cash was virtually inside, his curiosity working overtime.

I demonstrated Cash's new feat and rattled on about the learning process. The discovery of pressure and release.

"Have you tried that with his ears?" she asked.

Cash had come to us with one rule: *Do not ever touch my ears!*

We had often wondered what might've happened in the past to cause this reaction. I've heard of trainers who have been known to twist an ear to *make* a horse do or accept something. Whatever it was, we couldn't get close. Couldn't even scratch him between the ears.

"Good idea!" I said.

The *pressure*, in this instance, would come from his own fear of humans touching his ears.

I reached slowly up the side of his head toward his ear. He immediately pulled away when I got too close. My hand went with him, staying in position, creating even more pressure, until he stopped and held still for a couple of seconds. Until he was able to realize that it wasn't going to hurt him. Until he relaxed. Then I removed my hand.

It happened. He finally began to think, *This is no big deal.* That bought him a release of pressure. More comfort.

I reached again, a bit farther.

When he didn't retreat, I dropped my hand. The release of pressure sent a message, just as it had when releasing the halter while teaching him to lower his head.

One more time. Gaining an inch over the time before. And I retreated immediately when he didn't pull away.

And rubbed him on the forehead. *Good boy.*

And so it went, gaining an inch or so with each try. If he pulled away, I'd go with him until he relaxed. It didn't happen often. He was getting the picture.

It took about ten minutes before my fingers were wrapped around the base of his ear, rubbing very gently. Then withdrawing.

I quit for the day, feeling there had been a major breakthrough.

The next day, after maybe twenty minutes of micro progressions, I wound up with my hand wrapped all the way around his ear and my thumb rubbing gently *inside*.

Just amazing.

Approaching the other ear was not quite like starting at square-one, but close. By the end of the week, I could rub both ears, inside and out, and today Cash virtually purrs when we do this, leaning into it, saying, *More, more.*

It's truly exciting what a bit of understanding can do.

And patience.

That's the huge lesson Cash, and all the other horses, are teaching me. I've never been accused of having a lot of patience.

Not even a little.

Cash showed me the way.

Again.

Don't start halfway around the track, Joe. Start at the starting gate. Because when faced with an unruly horse, who hasn't begun at the beginning, a beast six or seven times your own weight, it's a knee-jerk reaction to attempt to overcome his enormous size with force and dominance.

I remember one of the first times I went on a trail ride. A mere kid, primed with decades of cowboy movies, my first goal was to let this huge creature know in no uncertain terms who was boss. Understand that this poor horse had probably been doing the same thing, dealing with idiots like me, day in and day out, for longer than I had been alive. But there I was, reins pulled tight, jerking this way and that, kicking his sides, establishing my dominance. Without a single clue.

The real embarrassment is that, decades later, when Kathleen arranged my birthday trail ride, I was doing exactly the same things. Establishing my bossmanship. Looking like I knew what I was doing. Soaking up compliments from the trail leader.

And in a way, I suppose, all of that's fine for the occasional trail rider. Most trail horses know so much more than those who ride them it's difficult to do too much wrong. They won't let you. They are turning, going, and stopping before you think about it so you don't have to jerk on their mouth or kick them in the side. The years have taught them.

But for the horse owner, there's only one place to begin.

At the beginning.

Stand in the horse's hooves. Study his history. Understand why he is the way he is, and why he acts the way he does.

He's a prey animal.

You mean like a rabbit??

Pretty much, yeah.

But he weighs eleven hundred pounds!!

Yep.

Discover what makes him feel safe. What keeps him healthy. What he wants in a leader. And why.

And then do it.

2

FEAR

The birthday trail ride that began our journey with horses was not something Kathleen was looking forward to. It was a gift for me. I was suffering from the so-so results of the last Benji movie and she had wanted to find something for my birthday that would be a diversion, and make me smile. I had no idea that she was petrified of horses. And I didn't learn about it for months. That's the way she is.

When her fears finally began to creep out of the closet, I became even more committed to making sure our new horses were safe, and our relationship with them well founded. Begin at the beginning. Take whatever time it takes.

Clinician John Lyons says that there is a real reason for fear. "Fear is recognition of loss of control, and it subsides when control returns," he says.

That's why so many of the DVDs and books begin with the art of gaining control of the horse's body parts. Moving them this way and that. Backward, forward, and sideways. Both on the ground and in the saddle. That control buys safety, and respect from the horse because you are speaking the language of the herd. Who moves who.

But looking back on Kathleen's fear, I would adjust John Lyons' phrase to read: Fear subsides when you *believe* that control has returned. Because all too often I would watch Kathleen do a splendid job of controlling her horse, only to find out later that she didn't *believe* she was in control. She was going through the motions, doing what the DVDs and books said, but she didn't believe she was actually leading the horse. There was no connection. She was merely executing a learned exercise without understanding the point of the exercise.

My fear threshold was much higher than Kathleen's, probably because at some unconscious level I was actually relating to the horses. Perhaps born from decades of work with dogs. Of living inside their hearts and souls trying to draw you in. When Cash walked up behind me and touched my shoulder in that first Join-Up, there was an emotional exchange. I gave absolute trust to him when I turned my back. He returned it when he touched me on the shoulder. I know now there was no such exchange when Kathleen did her first Join-Up. She went through the motions, but was petrified that the horse might walk up behind her and knock her down. Because she didn't understand – and thereby *believe* – the genetics and language of the herd. So there was no offering of trust. She knew it, and unfortunately, the horse knew it as well. As whacky as it might sound to anyone who hasn't been there, they do read these things. Unerringly. Horses will never be dishonest with you, and they will always know when you are dishonest with them.

When a horse has chosen a human to be his or her leader, along with that choice comes an implied responsibility to do what the leader asks. So long as the horse understands what the leader is asking. So long as the leader keeps the trust and respect of the horse. And so long as the horse feels he or she is safe with this leader.

Such a relationship does not dissipate just because the horse spends time with other horses. The human is now part of the social order.

I can walk in at any time and have a special moment with any of the horses. Even with halter and lead rope in hand. No one runs or hides. Often they'll come to me and follow me around. I'm not just one of the guys, I'm one of the *respected, trusted* guys. One of the *safe* guys. As is Kathleen. They know that whatever comes, it's not going to be bad, and will most likely be good. And we make sure that's the way it works out.

The leadership must be genuine, which for us has meant spending time with the herd absorbing the way they make decisions. How they discipline each other. And how all that translates into respect, and trust. For a while, this was difficult for Kathleen. As she worked her way through her fear, she would often try to fake it by yelling and waving her arms at the horses to assert herself, which she didn't realize, was really a step toward dominance. And it scared the horses.

"A leader doesn't act like a wild person," I finally told her. "All you need do is swell up like a horse and pin your ears."

"I can't pin my ears," she grumbled.

"Yes you can," I said. "Figuratively, you can. Watch."

I turned my back on Scribbles, who was always trying to invade our space, get close, nibble at my hat or shirt. And sure enough, here he came. I spun around and looked him straight in the eye, and swelled up like a hot air balloon. A flick of my finger and the words *back up,* said firmly but quietly, were all it took. He stopped in his tracks, and took two steps backward. I rubbed him on the forehead and scratched his ear.

"Good boy."

The next morning at feeding time, Kathleen worked the same magic on Mariah, who was always trying to steal Skeeter's feed from her. And she amazed even herself. That afternoon, when I couldn't find her, I wandered over to the pasture and there she was, in class. Soaking up the way the horses do it.

Leadership and respect do not come from bossmanship. And conversely it is not given to someone who showers horses with baskets full of love, without discipline. Sit and watch a herd sometime. Just watch. Make note of who respects whom, and how it's shown.

I respect you enough, and trust you enough, to subordinate my judgment and safety to you.

Pretty powerful when you know that, to the horse, safety means survival.

But I wouldn't learn most of this until further down the line. At the time I was just beginning to realize that something was amiss, for both of us. Kathleen was having trouble giving trust to receive it, so she was unable to actually *believe* she was in control. I knew I was in control, but had no idea why. And when logic is removed from any equation, it makes me crazy.

The following story is not mine. I asked and received permission from Monty Roberts to summarize it here because I feel it's so important to understand what can actually be accomplished. Monty has written an entire book on the subject entitled *Shy Boy*. I encourage you to read it.

Monty was asked by the BBC if he thought he could accomplish his *Join-Up* procedure totally in the wild. Without round pens, without lead lines. Just him and a wild horse. A mustang. He said yes, and a few months later he did just that. With cameras rolling, he *joined up* with a mustang in the wild, saddled, bridled, and placed a rider on the horse he later named Shy Boy. It took something like thirty-six hours to accomplish this feat. Monty was in the saddle of his own horse for most of that time. An amazing accomplishment. But the most important part of the story is this: A year later the BBC called again and asked Monty what he thought Shy Boy might do if he were returned to his herd. Would he choose to stay with the herd, or would he stay with Monty?

Frankly, Monty wasn't sure he wanted to find out. He now loved this horse. But persistence from TV producers convinced him. And, again with cameras rolling, they found the herd and released Shy Boy.

The mustang took one look at the herd and loped off to join them. They were last seen that evening, literally, racing off into the sunset. Monty stayed awake most of the night. He had lookouts positioned all over the place with radios, watching for the herd. Around nine o'clock the next morning, a radio crackled and blared that the herd was in sight, headed more or less their way. Shy Boy was out front.

At the bottom of the ridge that separated the horses from Monty's encampment, the herd stopped and Shy Boy climbed to the top of the ridge. He stood for quite some time looking first at the herd, then at the camp. Finally, he turned and galloped down the ridge toward the camp, weaving in and out of tall brush, slowing to a trot, then a walk, stopping only when he was nose-to-nose with Monty. I cried like a baby when I read that story. Imagine how you would feel if that was your horse, turned loose to make his own choice, to run free with his herd, or come back to you. You would surely know that you had been doing something right.

We were finally able to meet Monty about a year into our journey. It was a meeting at his ranch to discuss his possible involvement in an upcoming movie. But it was difficult for me to stay focused. This man is an icon in the horse world, and I had read his every book and seen all of his DVDs. I was mesmerized.

Just listening firsthand to Monty speak of his experiences, and twisting and pulling ideas with him made it a very special encounter. But the highlight of the day – sorry Monty - was meeting and being able to Join-Up with Shy Boy himself.

Seeing our twins, Allegra and Dylan, then twelve, Join-Up with this famous horse as if they had been doing it all their lives confirmed forever the simplicity and value of the process. They did a much better job than I did. With the master himself barking directions and correcting my body positions, I felt like a bumbling buffoon.

But Shy Boy made up for all of our shortcomings and was having a terrific time showing us the ropes. There was no question that this was one happy horse.

When he was turned back out into the wild, I am quite certain that there are trainers and horsemen galore to whom Shy Boy would've never returned.

But he returned to Monty Roberts.

I tell everyone Shy Boy's story. I tell it over and over again.

It's the way it should be. And it doesn't have to be any other way.

It's what happens when you begin at the beginning.

Which is the singular best way to completely eliminate fear from your experience with horses.

Relationship first.

Followed by good leadership.

And thoroughly understanding the whys and wherefores of both. Not just doing the exercises.

When you get both right you will have nothing to fear because you will have a safe and willing partner.

3

WHO MOVES WHO

Assume the predator stance. Swell up like a balloon. Eyes wide. Eyebrows up. Be a horse. A leader horse.

Now shake that lead rope and wag your finger at the same time.

"Back up! Back up!"

Some say that horses are not verbal so it's best not to give them verbal orders. Restrict the teaching to body language.

I say use everything you've got, especially in the beginning.

Shake the lead rope. Wag the finger. Say "Back up!"

Most clinicians and trainers agree that teaching your horse to back up is probably the best, single most influential maneuver you can teach him or her in the beginning.

Why?

Because most horses rarely back up on their own. They have only one distant blind spot in their field of vision and that spot is directly behind them. Being a prey animal, a flight animal, backing into the unknown would not be one of their favorite pastimes. So when you ask your horse to back up and he does so willingly it deeply implants and reaffirms his trust in you *and* your leadership.

Extended and/or fast *back ups* are very unnatural to the horse but once you've spent the time to get him to that point it can become so automatic that the exercise can be used anytime something freaks your horse or a gust of wind shoots his adrenaline through the roof. Asking him to "back up" will calm him down, cause him to get back to the thinking side of his brain instead of reactive side, and to focus again on you, not whatever is bugging him. And it's the quickest easiest way to move a horse out of your personal space if he's trying to jump into your pocket.

We studied and used Monty Roberts' Join Up for relationship. Then for leadership (ground work) we shuffled together Monty, Clinton Anderson, and Pat and Linda Parelli using a bit of this and a bit of that.

My personal favorite beginning method for teaching *back up* is Pat Parelli's beginning method because I believe it's the simplest for the horse to understand. I use a handy stick with its tip-end pressed into the horse's chest – Pat calls his a carrot stick - applying just enough backward pressure for it to be uncomfortable for the horse. Then I hold that pressure. The horse will eventually take a step backward to get away from the stick, to relieve the pressure. Instantaneously I release the pressure, rub the spot, and praise-praise-praise. That moment is when the horse learns. *Oh, I get it. If he touches my chest, and I back up, the pressure goes away. So he must want me to back up.*

I've also been known to annoyingly tap the horse's chest with the back of my hand or the handy stick until he steps backward away from the tapping. Then stop immediately and praise-praise-praise. Then do it again. And again. Graduating to two steps, then three, and ultimately however far I'd like him to go. Clinton backs his horses all the way from the paddock to the arena just for the practice.

Before I'm done I graduate to a finger in his chest, then just a flopping of my hands toward the horse's chest with the words "Back up, back up." Unlike most professional trainers I do want my horses to understand my words so I use them right from the beginning. I'm even teaching Cash conceptual thinking. I ask him to say hello by lifting and waving his foot. Whichever foot he waves, I then say, "Now the *other* foot" and he waves the opposite front. He understands "Up, up, up!" Used when his foot isn't high enough, or if I'm asking him to lift his head higher for a big smile. And now I can just walk toward him at liberty and say, "Back up... back up" and he'll back all the way to the next town. Well... maybe not, but you get the idea.

There are probably as many ways to teach the *back up* as there are clinicians and trainers. Which one you use is not as important as making sure you are actually communicating well with your horse. That he understands what you're wanting him to do. A horse who has chosen you in relationship and trusts you will pretty much do any reasonable thing that you'd like him to do *if* he clearly understands your wishes. It's never – or rarely if ever – an issue of the horse just not wanting to do it. It's virtually always an issue of trainer communication. So when it's not working, step back and take a look at what you're doing. Ask yourself if you were a horse would *you* understand that?

Probably the preferred back up method for most trainers is to shake the lead rope. After Parelli implants the *back up* concept with his carrot stick, he shifts to the lead rope, first merely wagging a finger, then if the horse doesn't back up – which none ever do at that point – he shakes the lead rope lightly for maybe a count of four, then, if necessary, more vigorously for another count, and then still more vigorously until the horse responds with just a single step backwards. Then pressure release, stop shaking the lead rope, praise him and give him a rub. I've used this method but personally find the combination described above to be understood more quickly by our horses. And I like to work without a rope, at liberty, any time possible. The ultimate goal of this method is to have your horse back up with a mere wag of your finger, eliminating the shaking lead rope altogether.

Some wave a handy stick in the horse's face like a windshield wiper and march toward the horse. If he doesn't step backward he gets whacked. I don't care for whacking.

Clinton taps the air just above the lead rope – four times. If the horse doesn't step back, he taps the rope four times, then taps it harder, then, if necessary, whacks the rope, using the philosophy: *as little as possible but as much as necessary*. Parelli whacks the ground instead of the lead rope and combines this with a wagging finger.

Monty Roberts uses his patented Dually Halter to teach backup and Kathleen and I worked with this method back in the very beginning when teaching our horses trailer loading. The halter has a piece of rope that tightens across the bridge of his nose when pressure is put on it. Sort of like a hackamore bridle. It causes no pain but is uncomfortable enough to cause the horse to step backward to release the pressure. Interestingly this was when I started using the words, "Back up, back up." The horses learned the words and associated them with stepping backwards, so later, when I tried other cues or signals, I received virtual immediate response.

Again, a horse well joined-up will almost always do what you ask once he understands what you're asking. My goal then is for you to understand this concept so well that you will do whatever it takes and spend as much time as necessary to figure out what you have to do to ensure that your communication with your horse is clear. Every horse is different. Every human is different. And every relationship is different. So that means lots of mileage to understand your horse so that you can teach him to understand you.

Like anything else in life, good communication is essential.

The next exercise I would attack is asking your horse to move his hindquarters left and right in a complete circle.

Why?

Because his hindquarters are his forward power, his engine. When he's moving those hindquarters left or right, crossing one leg in front of the other, his engine is shut down for all practical purposes. His forward power is out of balance. And just like backing up, when he willingly offers that to you his trust in you is ever deepening. Also, when you start riding, he is a much safer horse because you can take away his forward power anytime you want.

The way we began this exercise is, again, Pat Parelli's method and it's exactly like the back up. Place the carrot stick, end first, into his flank and apply pressure. The instant his hindquarters take a sideways step release the pressure, rub and praise. Then again, and again. Two steps, then three, and four, until his butt is moving in a full circle with the lightest of pressure. Then do the same thing on the other side moving the other way. Then, finally, do it all with just a look and a point with the stick. No touching. And ultimately, just a point with your finger. Or just a look.

Being the vocabulary builder I am, I also use words with this exercise. "Move butt." It helps me communicate with them as I ease off the stick pressure and try other signals.

Next, for us, was moving the forequarters left and right in a complete circle. And we began, again as Pat does, with pressure from the stick (or a finger) in the soft area right behind the horse's jaw bone. Just enough to be uncomfortable. Then hold it until the horse takes a sideways step. Then, as before, two steps, three steps, etc. Ultimately graduating to whatever non-touching gesture you prefer. I use the words, "Move over." Or "Out of my way please." They have all come to know the basic meaning of the words "Out" and "Over." But be consistent in the beginning and only begin adlibbing once they fully grasp the exercise.

Our preferred method of beginning to teach the horse to come forward with the lead rope is Parelli's. Start stroking the lead rope as if you were pulling on it but without pulling. Wear a big happy welcoming smile (opposite of your *back up* pinned ears). If the horse doesn't come begin to squeeze the rope a bit, just a little pressure. Then squeeze harder until you are actually applying pressure. If the horse still has not taken a forward step, then pull just hard enough to balance the resistance from the horse and hold that pressure. Eventually the horse *will* take a step forward to remove the pressure. Release, rub and praise. Then start over. At two weeks old it only took our Malachi two or three tries at this before he got it completely. From that point forward, whenever I combed the lead rope he would come to me. When I took a step he took a step.

So you are well on your way. You are moving your horse forward, backward, left and right, front and back. Thus you are, by his choice, his leader. He confirms that fact every time he backs up for you, or moves his butt, or follows along side on the lead rope. Who moves who... is you.

Leadership confirmed.

As mentioned earlier I'm not a professional trainer. But by the grace of God we got started right and because of the changes that relationship brought to our lives I became obsessed with understanding what makes our horses tick. I spent an enormous amount of time with the horses, and reading books, and watching DVDs. And ultimately, more or less working backwards, put together some truths about our horses that have made their lives and ours so much better.

My fondest hope is that this book will provide you with discoveries and concepts that will make your journey with horses better. I thank those who have helped us along the way, and hope that in passing along what we've learned from them we are helping you.

Pat Parelli intrinsically knows and understands more about horses than any of us probably ever will. Perhaps all of us put together. And I love watching him just to know what's possible. His 17-minute demonstration teaching Games 2, 3, and 4 to a new untrained horse on DVD #2 of their Level 1 Kit was worth the price of the entire set. Soak this man up anytime you can.

It's sad that Clinton Anderson does not begin with relationship first (except with his own personal horses) but I feel he is one of the best teachers around, especially if you're a 1-2-3 kind of learner. His basic ground work fundamentals are effective, precise, clear, and simple to understand and execute. Check out his DVDs on Downunder Horsemanship and especially his book Lessons Well Learned (this is an Amazon link where it's much less expensive). If only he chose to begin with relationship like Monty and Pat Parelli his job would be so much easier and the horses would be much more willing.

As mentioned earlier, we used Monty Robert's Join-Up to establish our relationship with each horse and it has made all the difference. Had we not stumbled onto him even before our first horse arrived, there probably never would've been a book entitled *The Soul of a Horse*. His understanding of the horse's language and his Join-Up method of causing a horse to accept and trust you of his own free will in only 15 to 20 minutes blew me away and it immediately became our way for every one of our horses. His trailer loading teaching is simply amazing and that's how all of our herd learned. And Monty's Equus Online University is probably the best equine educational value out there on the internet. You can watch any and every lesson any-time you choose to, in any order, for less than $10/month. And there's a new lesson every week.

There are tons of additional trainers and clinicians out there, many of them terrific in what they do and teach. The above three are the ones who gave breath and life to our journey with horses. Our wish for you is simply that you choose whichever ones help you learn to communicate well with your horse without becoming addicted to any one method or technique. Mix them together and spend the mileage until you are able to figure things out for yourself and trust yourself to take a deep breath and let your horse be your teacher.

4

DOES IT WORK?

"Back up! Back up!"

Sojourn took a step backward and I dropped the pressure immediately. Release from pressure equals reward. Reward equals learning.

This was one scary horse. Not because he wanted to be. Not because he was mean. Because he was *big!* And he was very smart. And I was very new to all this.

And, unlike any other horse we'd met, he was very possessive. He wanted *all* of my time. *All* the time. But he was only one of four, soon to be one of six. I was beginning to wonder if Join-Up had worked too well? Was the bond too strong?

Because he was so bright, he became bored easily and would destroy virtually anything in his stall just to have something to do. This was before we discovered that stalls and horses were an unhealthy mix. Sojourn was trying to tell us something.

His relationship with the other horses also left much to be desired. He would become upset when anyone else received attention. He's the one I allowed Cash to be stalled with, which resulted in a gashing kick to Cash's forehead. It was becoming a problem.

Still I persisted, working on leadership, doing lots of ground work. *Back up. Move your hindquarters. Come in. Go this way. Now the other way.* He listened well and began to learn, and was quite willing to stay in the arena all day. *Never mind those other nags* I could almost hear him saying. *I'm your man.*

Very soon it became apparent that no one else in the family wanted anything to do with Sojourn. Other than to rub him… from across the fence. I was the only one who would work with him, and, frankly, I rather enjoyed seeing the progress with such a high-strung, possessive horse. But he was keeping me away from Cash and the other horses.

He was one of our first three horses, and a perfect example of what *not* to do when looking for a horse. He was young, gorgeous, very athletic, and would hang with you like a puppy.

Awww, he loves me already. Look, he wants to be my buddy.

This was before I knew that *buddy* was defined differently within the herd. Before I had learned how valuable it can be to spend time with the horses, just observing the language, the interaction. Before I had discovered that a strong and effective relationship with a horse required, in effect, the human to become one. And before I knew how carefully one's first horse should be selected. This was back in the beginning, and I had a lot to learn.

A lot.

This was also before I knew that I could search deeply into a horse's eyes and actually feel what was going on inside. Is this a kind horse? A gentle horse? Is it a willing horse? Will he accept a leader easily? All of that was yet to come. With experience. And lots of time in the pasture. As was the knowledge that we couldn't rely on sellers to tell us what we were not experienced enough to see.

But I did know how to get this horse onto the thinking side of his brain. Give him a task, or stir his curiosity. Divert him from the reactive side. And keep the adrenaline down. His, and mine.

Sojourn was smart but didn't seem to want to be bothered with the basic tasks. I believe he figured he could take fine care of himself, thank you, and what was the point of all this anyway? Maintaining a leadership position with him was eating up all of my time. What I didn't know then is that he was teaching me a very valuable lesson.

It wasn't long before Kathleen and I began to nibble at the edges of putting Sojourn up for sale.

"I don't think so," I said. "He's gonna be a great horse. He has a lot of issues, but I can do this. I can bring him along."

"At what price to the other horses? At what price to your own learning curve?"

It was a conundrum. I actually liked him a lot. But he and I didn't have the connection that Cash and I had. It was just different, and difficult to explain.

I wanted to be with Cash.

I enjoyed being with Cash.

I wanted to *teach* Sojourn. The primary enjoyment from the relationship was seeing thresholds give way to progress. I suppose if he hadn't demanded so much of my time, it could've been different. But the mission was becoming a chore and really began to wear on me.

"He needs someone who only wants one horse, one focus," Kathleen admonished one morning over cappuccino. We were watching the horses pace back and forth in their cute little stalls. "Someone who will fill his day and spend time only with him."

"I know. I know. But that would be like giving up. Like failing."

One of my scorpions.

I do hate to fail.

Mistakes, unfortunately, are a natural consequence of doing. The only way to avoid mistakes is to do nothing. When you're trying new things, taking risks, pushing for perfection, moving the ball forward you're going to take some hits. The challenge is to go ahead and take the hits, admit the mistake, swallow the pride, use it as a learning experience, climb back onto your feet, and move forward.

"I can't sell him," I said.

Kathleen sighed.

"You're becoming obsessive about this. You know that, right?"

Of course I knew it. But I didn't nod. I think *pout* would've been the operative word.

"So what if you do cause Sojourn to be the lightest, most receptive, most responsive horse in the state, what then? You don't care anything about competing. And you're never going to leave Cash. You enjoy him too much. So what then? You'll either have to keep up the training to prevent him from slipping backward, or you'll sell him to someone who'll appreciate him. Why not do that now?"

I studied on that for some time, then:

"Because he's so big he scares me," I finally admitted. "I'm afraid to ride him, and I need to get over that."

That wasn't easy. Males aren't supposed to admit fear. I knew Kathleen had fears, but until that moment, she had no clue that I did as well.

"I suspect you're afraid because you don't believe your riding skills are good enough for Sojourn yet. And that makes him the wrong horse to learn on. I would think you should learn on a horse that makes you feel comfortable. You cannot concentrate on teaching the horse or yourself while fear is running out your ears."

Where have I heard that before? Or rather, where would I hear it again, months later? Foreshadowing.

"Don't hammer me with logic," I said. "It's not fair."

Kathleen smiled.

The decision was made, but I can't say that I was ever 100 percent in favor of it. Consent was all tangled up in my feelings for Sojourn, along with a smidgen of ego, the notion of failure, and the fact that we had no idea where this journey was taking us. By this point, I was reasonably certain that something was up. That God was leading us down this trail for a reason. But, unfortunately, God has never felt obliged to keep us apprised of His intentions.

Seven months after bringing Sojourn to our place, we decided to deliver him to our benevolent horse broker friend. Horses are her business. She is very picky and always makes sure the match between buyer and horse is a good one. If she didn't like the buyer, she would not recommend a sale. This was the same woman who had presented Cash to us. We told her that Sojourn must go to a good, kind home with an owner for whom Sojourn would be the only horse. Not a one-horse household. But a one-person horse. It saddens me to note that he still wore metal shoes because we had not yet reached the barefoot junction of our journey.

Meanwhile, the decision to sell fueled other problems.

We had to move him over to his interim home. And that meant we had to finally use our trailer.

The trailer we had raced out to buy one short month after the first three horses came to live with us.

"Why do we need a trailer now?" Kathleen had pleaded. "We don't even know what we're doing with these horses yet."

"You never know," I said. "You never know when we might need it."

I thought at the time that perhaps the scariest moment of my life was pulling our new gooseneck three-horse-plus-tack-room trailer back home from the dealer. It wasn't. The scariest moment was getting this twenty-nine-foot monstrosity up our driveway, then a three hundred-foot vertical rise from top to bottom that seemed to go straight up in spots. One of the steepest points was a hairpin turn, at least 270 degrees, through a gate!

For reasons that carry no more logic than my original belief that horses should wear shoes, it had never occurred to me that the trailer might not make it up the driveway, through the gate, and around the turn. That thought hit me about halfway home. Suddenly, pulling the trailer down a traffic-logged California freeway was no longer an issue. I was terrified that I would get halfway up the driveway and that would be it. Our new used 2001 Dodge 2500 pickup would just quit. It was not four-wheel drive. Why? Don't even ask. For inexplicable reasons, my car is, but the pickup acquired to pull this huge trailer isn't.

If we had to stop for the gate to open, would we be able to start up again? And could we make the hairpin turn, which would have to be done very slowly to be certain the trailer didn't trash the gate trying to squeeze through? And if it *did* go through and made the turn, would it continue up the steepest part?

The good news is that the truck performed valiantly and the trailer missed the gate with at least two inches to spare. The bad news is that the trailer sat at the top of the hill for seven months before it ever moved again. I suspect I was more afraid of the trailer and the driveway than I was of riding Sojourn.

"So tell me again why we needed this trailer way back in June?" Kathleen asked often.

"Er… uh… practice?" I would squeak.

Practice was actually a pretty good answer. It didn't address the reason why the trailer hadn't moved in half a year, but having it had enabled us to learn a new skill. Before purchasing the trailer, we had never loaded a horse, *any* horse, into any trailer.

All of our horses responded differently to the experience.

Some acted as if they had never seen a trailer before. Others – Cash – walked right in and started chomping hay.

With Join-Up, and Monty Roberts' trailering techniques, what apparently can often be a very stressful time for man and horse went very well for us. When the

horse trusts and respects you as his leader, he is willing
to try uncomfortable tasks. In its simplest form, after
the horse is taught to back up, Monty teases him with
the trailer, walking him up to the door, and then backing him off. *Nope, we don't want to go in that big old nas-
ty trailer yet. No sir, we won't make you do that. But let's
go up and have another look.*

The horse is walked back up to the door again, giv-
en a moment to sniff and look, then backed away again.
Over and over this happens. Again and again. Until finally you can actually feel the horse *wanting* to go in.
No more backups please! At that moment, Monty keeps
walking right into the trailer and most horses follow
him right in. Those who don't go back to the beginning
and do some more backing up. It's fascinating to watch,
but even more fascinating to see how well it worked
with our own horses.

All six of ours wound up going into the trailer quite
willingly, happily, within a few hours at the most. Not
one was ever forced, even a little. The choice was always
theirs. Even with Sojourn.

Pocket gave us one of my favorite memories of these lessons. The first time I stepped into the trailer asking her to follow, she stopped short, looked at me for a
moment, and stood straight up on her hind legs! A full
blown Roy Rogers-and-Trigger kind of rear. No paw-
ing the air. No intent to harm. Just saying, *I don't want
to do that just yet.*

I stood there with a silly grin spread across my face, less than ten feet away from this big paint horse who was suddenly about twelve feet tall. *This is going to take a while*, I thought. But I couldn't have been more wrong. I backed her away once, then walked up and stepped into the trailer and she practically ran over me coming in behind. No resistance whatsoever. Go figure.

The day we loaded Sojourn to move him, the emotions were not as happy, and I'm sure he was reading our mood because he was clearly a bit tense. He walked right into the trailer and I closed the partition. But when I closed the trailer door with no other horses in the trailer, he became seriously fidgety and pawed the floor. As we drove out right past the other horses and his one herd buddy, I could hear him stomping around and calling to his herd mates, which did nothing to settle my nerves, already scrambled from the decision to sell, and from navigating my first trip down the driveway with an actual passenger in the trailer.

It was less than a fifteen-minute ride, but I was very relieved when we arrived. As I opened the door, Sojourn became more agitated. To say I was nervous would be an understatement. This would be a test of will to keep my adrenaline down. The trailer looked much smaller now than it had in the past. When I opened the partition, it would be just me and that gigantic horse in this tiny little trailer. A gigantic horse who was clearly not very happy about something. I had no idea about what until the partition swung open.

His front right foot was caught in the hay bag, about chest high.

He was terrified. He couldn't get away from it. When the partition swung open, he wanted to bolt, but couldn't. He was tugging and stomping, and trying to rear enough to get his foot out. Should I run? Get out of harm's way? Should I try to calm him and get close enough to unsnap the feed bag? That option didn't seem very intelligent at the moment. I swelled up like Jabba the Hut, shook the lead rope, and wagged my finger in his face.

"Back up," I said, as if he could. "Easy."

I was trying to control my own adrenaline. All of this happened so furiously fast that I have no idea how or why I decided to throw caution to the wind in favor of trying to make him focus on a task, get out of the reactive side of his brain, and, hopefully, get calm enough for me to approach his foot and unsnap the feed bag.

Outside the trailer, Kathleen was frozen in place, afraid to even think of looking inside. She was certain from the stomping she heard that I was being trampled to death. At some level I suppose I had considered that possibility but had decided that I would attempt to rise above it. Do whatever had to be done and do it well enough to make it work. To keep both myself and Sojourn safe from injury. I'd worry about what could've happened later.

Inside, Sojourn's eyes were as big as saucers. All I could see was white, but he was watching me. He seemed to be listening. Or trying to. Then suddenly the feed bag tore loose and his foot was free. This could be good, or it could be terrible. I shook the lead rope harder, wagging my finger at light speed.

"Easy. Good boy. Back up. Just a bit. Pay attention to me."

My adrenaline wanted to soar, but amazingly didn't. I could *feel* the calm, the lid staying on. I knew this was the answer. If I was calm, I had a shot at causing Sojourn to be calm. He was blowing and snorting, his eyes still crazed, but he was standing still, more or less. He was listening to me. I eased toward the door, consciously deciding whether to toss the rope and let him bolt or step in front of him and rely on my ability to keep him calm. Relatively speaking.

I chose the latter. I stopped him. Backed him up a step, which he accepted. Then I slid in front of him and stepped cleanly out the door and immediately to my right, out of his way. He came right out behind me and loped off to the end of the lead rope. I signaled him to come in rather than walking to him, wanting to keep him focused, thinking. He huffed and puffed and snorted, but walked slowly up to me and I rubbed his forehead.

"Good boy," I said. "*Very* good boy."

I had never meant anything more in my life.

I was so proud of him. And of myself. And of the fact that this event, as traumatic as it was for Sojourn, me, and Kathleen, would forever live as the certain proof that all we believed and all we were doing was right and good. That when a horse has entered relationship with us of his own free choice and trusts us to be his herd leader, and when we accept and live up to that position, he will defer. He will subordinate even his worst fears to the trust he has placed in us.

When Kathleen finally tiptoed up to us, tears were running down my cheeks.

"Did you see that?" I blubbered.

"I did."

Did you see how good he was?"

"I did."

She rubbed him on the forehead.

"I can't leave him here," I said.

"You also can't do it all," she said. "And he wants it all."

She let that sink in for a moment.

"Our decision is a good one," she said. "He needs a full-time leader. You've done an amazing job with him, and he has taught you that the sky is truly the limit when you walk in the horses' footsteps, when they make the choice, and when you fulfill their need for trust and leadership. He proved the truth of that today in spades, and we can love him for it. But remember, part of loving, the hard part, is making sure that he has what he needs. Sojourn needs someone else. And our other horses need you."

It was a quiet ride home. For once I wasn't thinking about the big trailer that was following us.

"It's interesting," I said, "how a single thought or event can feel both good and bad, can cause hurt and yet empower."

"Yes it is," Kathleen said. "It is indeed."

Neither of us spoke again. We were thinking about Sojourn. And the legacy he had left us.

We now knew it was all for real. It was all true.

Good boy, Sojourn.

The above chapter is an edited excerpt from the best selling book The Soul of a Horse – Life Lessons from the Herd by Joe Camp published by Harmony Books.

Follow Joe & Kathleen's Journey
From no horses and no clue to stumbling through mistakes, fear, fascination and frustration on a collision course with the ultimate discovery that something was very wrong in the world of horses.

Read the National Best Seller
The Soul of a Horse
Life Lessons from the Herd

…and the Highly Acclaimed Best Selling Sequel

Born Wild
The Soul of a Horse

The above links and all of the links that follow are live links in the eBook editions available at Amazon Kindle, Barnes & Noble Nook, Google Play, and Apple iBooks

WHAT READERS AND CRITICS ARE SAYING ABOUT JOE CAMP

"Joe Camp is a master storyteller." *THE NEW YORK TIMES*

"Joe Camp is a gifted storyteller and the results are magical. Joe entertains, educates and empowers, baring his own soul while articulating keystone principles of a modern revolution in horsemanship." *RICK LAMB, AUTHOR AND TV/RADIO HOST "THE HORSE SHOW"*

"This book is fantastic. It has given me shivers, made me laugh and cry, and I just can't seem to put it down!" *CHERYL PANNIER, WHO RADIO AM 1040 DES MOINES*

"One cannot help but be touched by Camp's love and sympathy for animals and by his eloquence on the subject." *MICHAEL KORDA, THE WASHINGTON POST*

"Joe Camp is a natural when it comes to understanding how animals tick and a genius at telling us their story. His books are must-reads for those who love animals of any species." *MONTY ROBERTS, AUTHOR OF NEW YORK TIMES BEST-SELLER THE MAN WHO LISTENS TO HORSES*

"Camp has become something of a master at telling us what can be learned from animals, in this case specifically horses, without making us realize we have been educated, and, that is, perhaps, the mark of a real teacher. The tightly written, simply designed, and powerfully drawn chapters often read like short stories that flow from the heart." *JACK L. KENNEDY, THE JOPLIN INDEPENDENT*

"This book is absolutely fabulous! An amazing, amazing book. You're going to love it." *JANET PARSHALL'S AMERICA*

"Joe speaks a clear and simple truth that grabs hold of your heart." *YVONNE WELZ, EDITOR, THE HORSE'S HOOF MAGAZINE*

"I wish you could *hear* my excitement for Joe Camp's new book. It is unique, powerful, needed." *DR. MARTY BECKER, BEST-SELLING AUTHOR OF SEVERAL CHICKEN SOUP FOR THE SOUL BOOKS AND POPULAR VETERINARY CONTRIBUTOR TO ABC'S GOOD MORNING AMERICA*

"I got my book yesterday and hold Joe Camp responsible for my bloodshot eyes. I couldn't put it down and morning came early!!! Joe transports me into his words. I feel like I am right there sharing his experiences. And his love for not just horses, but all of God's critters pours out from every page." *RUTH SWANDER – READER*

"I love this book! It is so hard to put it down, but I also don't want to read it too fast. I don't want it to end! Every person who loves an animal must have this book. I can't wait for the next one !!!!!!!!!" *NINA BLACK REID – READER*

"I LOVED the book! I had it read in 2 days. I had to make myself put it down. Joe and Kathleen have brought so much light to how horses should be treated and cared for. Again, thank you!" *ANITA LARGE - READER*

"LOVE the new book... reading it was such an emotional journey. Joe Camp is a gifted writer." *MARYKAY THUL LONGACRE - READER*

"I was actually really sad, when I got to the last page, because I was looking forward to picking it up every night." SABINE REYNOSO - READER

"*The Soul of a Horse Blogged* is insightful, enlightening, emotionally charged, hilarious, packed with wonderfully candid photography, and is masterfully woven by a consummate storyteller. Wonderful reading!" HARRY H. MACDONALD - READER

"I simply love the way Joe Camp writes. He stirs my soul. This is a must read book for everyone." DEBBIE K - READER

"This book swept me away. From the first to last page I felt transported! It's clever, witty, inspiring and a very fast read. I was sad when I finished it because I wanted to read more!" DEBBIE CHARTRAND – READER

"This book is an amazing, touching insight into Joe and Kathleen's personal journey that has an even more intimate feel than Joe's first best seller." KATHERINE BOWEN – READER

Also by Joe Camp

The National Best Seller
The Soul of a Horse
Life Lessons from the Herd

The Highly Acclaimed Best Selling Sequel
Born Wild
The Soul of a Horse

Amazon # 1
Horses & Stress
Eliminating the Root Cause of Most Health, Hoof & Behavior Problems

Amazon # 1
Why Relationship First Works
Why and How It Changes Everything

Training with Treats
With Relationship and Basic Training Locked In
Treats Can Be an Excellent Way to Enhance Good Communication

Why Our Horses Are Barefoot
Everything We've Learned About the Health and Happiness of the Hoof

God Only Knows
Can You Trust Him with the Secret?

The Soul of a Horse Blogged
The Journey Continues

Horses Were Born To Be On Grass
How We Discovered the Simple But Undeniable
Truth About Grass, Sugar, Equine Diet & Lifestyle

Horses Without Grass
How We Kept Six Horses Moving and Eating Happily
Healthily on an Acre and a Half of Rocks and Dirt

Who Needs Hollywood
The Amazing Story of How Benji Became the #3 Movie of the Year

Dog On It
Everything You Need To Know About Life Is Right There At Your Feet

RESOURCES

Watch the Video
Joe and Cash: Relationship First!
The Soul of a Horse Channel on YouTube

There are, I'm certain, many programs and people who subscribe to these philosophies and are very good at what they do but are not listed in these resources. That's because we haven't experienced them, and we will only recommend to you programs that we believe, from our own personal experience, to be good for the horse and well worth the time and money.

Monty Roberts and Join up:

http://www.montyroberts.com- Please start here! Or at Monty's Equus Online University which is terrific and probably the best Equine learning value out there on the internet (Watch the Join-Up lesson <u>and</u> the Special Event lesson. Inspiring!). This is where you get the relationship right with your horse. Where you learn to give him the choice of whether or not to trust you. Where everything changes when he does. Please, do this. Learn Monty's Join-Up method, either from his Online University, his books, or DVDs. Watching his *Join-Up* DVD was probably our single most pivotal experience in our very short journey with horses. Even if you've owned your horse forever, go back to the beginning and execute a Join Up with your horse or horses. You'll find that when you unconditionally offer choice to your horse and he chooses you, everything changes. You become a member of the herd, and your horse's leader, and with that goes responsibility on his part as well as yours. Even if you don't own horses, it is absolutely fascinating to watch Monty put a saddle and a rider on a completely unbroken horse in less than thirty minutes (unedited!). We've also watched and used Monty's *Dually Training Halter* DVD and his *Load-Up trailering* DVD. And we loved his books: *The Man Who Listens to Horses, The Horses in My Life, From My Hands to Yours, and Shy Boy.* Monty is a very impressive man who cares a great deal for horses.

http://www.imagineahorse.com- This is Allen Pogue and Suzanne De Laurentis' site. I cannot recommend strongly enough that everyone who leaves this eBook Nugget ready to take the next step with treats and vocabulary should visit this site and start collecting Allen's DVDs (he also sells big red circus balls). Because of his liberty work with multiple horses Allen has sort of been cast as a trick trainer, but he's so much more than that. It's all about relationship and foundation. We are dumbfounded by how Allen's horses treat him and try for him. His work with newborn foals and young horses is so logical and powerful that you should study it even if you never intend to own a horse. Allen says, "With my young horses, by the time they are three years old they are so mentally mature that saddling and riding is absolutely undramatic." He has taken Dr. Robert M. Miller's book *Imprint Training of the Newborn Foal* to a new and exponential level.

Frederick Pignon – This man is amazing and has taken relationship and bond with his horses to an astounding new level. Go to this link: (http://www.youtube.com/watch?v=w1YO3j-Zh3g) and watch the video of his show with three beautiful black Lusitano stallions, all at liberty. This show would border on the miraculous if they were all geldings, but they're not. They're stallions. Most of us will never achieve the level of bond Frederick has achieved with his horses but it's inspiring to know that it's possible, and to see what the horse-human relationship is capable of becoming. Frederick believes in true partnership with his horses, he believes in making every training session fun not work, he encourages the horses to offer their ideas, and he uses treats. When Kathleen read his book *Gallop to Freedom* her response to me was simply, "Can we just move in with them?"

<u>**Natural Horsemanship**</u>: This is the current buzz word for those who train horses or teach humans the training of horses without any use of fear, cruelty, threats, ag-

gression, or pain. The philosophy is growing like wild-fire, and why shouldn't it? If you can accomplish everything you could ever hope for with your horse and still have a terrific relationship with him or her, and be respected as a leader, not feared as a dominant predator, why wouldn't you? As with any broadly based general philosophy, there are many differing schools of thought on what is important and what isn't, what works well and what doesn't. Which of these works best for you, I believe, depends a great deal on how you learn, and how much reinforcement and structure you need. In our beginnings, we more or less shuffled together Monty Roberts (above) and the next two whose web-sites are listed below, favoring one source for this and another for that. But beginning with Monty's Join-Up. Often, this gave us an opportunity to see how different programs handle the same topic, which enriches insight. But, ultimately, they all end up at the same place: When you have a good relationship with your horse that began with choice, when you are respected as your horse's leader, when you truly care for your horse, then, before too long, you will be able to figure out for yourself the best communication to evoke any particular objective. These programs, as written, or taped on DVD, merely give you a structured format to follow that will take you to that goal.

http://www.parelli.com- Pat and Linda Parelli
have turned their teaching methods into a fully
accredited college curriculum. We have four of
their home DVD courses: *Level 1, Level 2, Level
3,* and *Liberty & Horse Behavior.* We recommend them all, but especially the first three. Often, they do run on, dragging out points much
longer than perhaps necessary, but we've found,
particularly in the early days, that knowledge
gained through such saturation always bubbles
up to present itself at the most opportune mo-
ments. In other words, it's good. Soak it up. It'll
pay dividends later. Linda is a good instructor,
especially in the first three programs, and Pat is
one of the most amazing horsemen I've ever
seen. His antics are inspirational for me. Not
that I will ever duplicate any of them, but knowing that it's possible is very affirming. And
watching him with a newborn foal is just fantastic. The difficulty for us with *Liberty & Horse
Behavior* (besides its price) is on disk 5 whereon
Linda consumes almost three hours to load an
inconsistent horse into a trailer. Her belief is
that the horse should *not* be *made* to do anything, he should *discover* it on his own. I believe
there's another option. As Monty Roberts
teaches, there is a big difference between *making*
a horse do something and *leading* him through

it, showing him that it's okay, that his trust in you is valid. Once you have joined up with him, and he trusts you, he is willing to take chances for you because of that trust, so long as you don't abuse the trust. On Monty's trailer-loading DVD Monty takes about one-tenth the time, and the horse (who was impossible to load before Monty) winds up loading himself from thirty feet away, happily, even playfully. And his trust in Monty has progressed as well, because he reached beyond his comfort zone and learned it was okay. His trust was confirmed. One thing the Parelli program stresses, in a way, is a followup to Monty Roberts' Join-Up: you should spend a lot of time just hanging out with your horse. In the stall, in the pasture, wherever. Quality time, so to speak. No agenda, just hanging out. Very much a relationship enhancer. And don't ever stomp straight over to your horse and slap on a halter. Wait. Let your horse come to you. It's that choice thing again, and Monty or Pat and Linda Parelli can teach you how it works.

http://www.chrislombard.com/ - An amazing horseman and wonderful teacher. His DVD *Beginning with the Horse* puts relationship, leadership and trust into simple easy-to-understand terms.

http://www.downunderhorsemanship.com-
This is Clinton Anderson's site. Whereas the Parellis are very philosophically oriented, Clinton gets down to business with lots of detail and repetition. What exactly do I do to get my horse to back up? From the ground and from the saddle, he shows you precisely, over and over again. And when you're in the arena or round pen and forget whether he used his left hand or right hand, or whether his finger was pointing up or down, it's very easy to go straightaway to the answer on his DVDs. His programs are very task-oriented, and, again, there are a bunch of them. We have consumed his *Gaining Respect and Control on the Ground, Series I through III* and *Riding with Confidence, Series I through III*. All are multiple DVD sets, so there has been a lot of viewing and reviewing. For the most part, his tasks and the Parellis are much the same, though usually approached very differently. Both have served a purpose for us. We also loved his *No Worries Tying DVD* for use with his Australian Tie Ring, which truly eliminates pull-back problems in minutes! And on this one he demonstrates terrific desensitizing tech-

niques. Clinton is the only two-time winner of the Road to the Horse competition, in which three top natural-horsemanship clinicians are given unbroken horses and a mere three hours to be riding and performing specified tasks. Those DVDs are terrific! And Clinton's Australian accent is also fun to listen to... mate.

The three programs above have built our natural horsemanship foundation, and we are in their debt. The following are a few others you should probably check out, each featuring a highly respected clinician, and all well known for their care and concern for horses.

http://www.robertmmiller.com - Dr. Robert M. Miller is an equine veterinarian and world renowned speaker and author on horse behavior and natural horsemanship. I think his name comes up more often in these circles than anyone else's. His first book, *Imprint Training of the Newborn Foal* is now a bible of the horse world. He's not really a trainer, per se, but a phenomenal resource on horse behavior. He will show you the route to "the bond." You must visit his website.

<u>Taking Your Horse Barefoot:</u> Taking your horses barefoot involves more than just pulling shoes. The new breed of natural hoof care practitioners have studied and rely completely on what they call the wild horse trim, which replicates the trim that horses give to themselves in the wild through natural wear. The more the domesticated horse is out and about, moving constantly, the less trimming he or she will need. The more stall-bound the horse, the more trimming will be needed in order to keep the hooves healthy and in shape. Every horse is a candidate to live as nature intended. The object is to maintain their hooves as if they were in the wild, and that requires some study. Not a lot, but definitely some. I now consider myself capable of keeping my horses' hooves in shape. I don't do their regular trim, but I do perform interim touch-ups. The myth that domesticated horses *must* wear shoes has been proven to be pure hogwash. The fact that shoes degenerate the health of the hoof and the entire horse has not only been proven, but is also recognized even by those who nail shoes on horses. Successful high performance barefootedness with the wild horse trim can be accomplished for virtually every horse on the planet, and the process has even been proven to be a healing procedure for horses with laminitis and founder. On this subject, I beg you not to wait. Dive into the material below and give your horse a longer, healthier, happier life.

http://www.hoofrehab.com/– This is Pete Ramey's website. If you read only one book on this entire subject, read Pete's *Making Natural Hoof Care Work for You*. Or better yet, get his DVD series *Under the Horse*, which is fourteen-plus hours of terrific research, trimming, and information. He is my hero! He has had so much experience with making horses better. He cares so much about every horse that he helps. And all of this comes out in his writing and DVD series. If you've ever doubted the fact that horses do not need metal shoes and are in fact better off without them, please go to Pete's website. He will convince you otherwise. Then use his teachings to guide your horses' venture into barefootedness. He is never afraid or embarrassed to change his opinion on something as he learns more from his experiences. Pete's writings have also appeared in *Horse & Rider* and are on his website. He has taken all of Clinton Anderson's horses barefoot.

The following are other websites that contain good information regarding the barefoot subject:

http://www.TheHorsesHoof.com– this website and magazine of Yvonne and James Welz is devoted entirely to barefoot horses around the world and is surely the single largest resource for owners, trimmers, case histories, and virtually everything you would ever want to know about barefoot horses. With years and years of barefoot experience, Yvonne is an amazing resource. She can compare intelligently this method vs that and help you to understand all there is to know. And James is a super barefoot trimmer.

http://www.wholehorsetrim.com - This is the website of Eddie Drabek, another one of my heroes. Eddie is a wonderful trimmer in Houston, Texas, and an articulate and inspirational educator and spokesman for getting metal shoes off horses. Read everything he has written, including the pieces on all the horses whose lives he has saved by taking them barefoot.

Our current hoof specialist in Tennessee is Mark Taylor who works in Tennessee, Arkansas, Alabama, and Mississippi 662-224-4158 http://www.barefoothorsetrimming.com/

http://www.aanhcp.net- This is the website for the American Association of Natural Hoof Care Practioners.

Also see: **the video of Joe: Why Are Our Horses Barefoot? On** The Soul of a Horse Channel on YouTube.

Natural Boarding: Once your horses are barefoot, please begin to figure out how to keep them out around the clock, day and night, moving constantly, or at least having that option. It's really not as difficult as you might imagine, even if you only have access to a small piece of property. Every step your horse takes makes his hooves and his body healthier, his immune system better. And it really is not that difficult or expensive to figure it out. Much cheaper than barns and stalls.

> **Paddock Paradise: A Guide to Natural Horse Boarding** This book by Jaime Jackson begins with a study of horses in the wild, then describes many plans for getting your horses out 24/7, in replication of the wild. The designs are all very specific, but by reading the entire book you begin to deduce what's really important and what's not so important, and why. We didn't follow any of his plans, but we have one pasture that's probably an acre and a half and two much smaller ones (photos on our website www.thesoulofahorse.com). All of them function very well when combined with random food placement. They keep our horses on the move, as they would be in the wild. The big one

is very inexpensively electrically-fenced. *Paddock Paradise* is available, as are all of Jaime's books, at **http://www.paddockparadise.com/**

Also see the video **The Soul of a Horse Paddock Paradise: What We Did, How We Did It, and Why** on The Soul of a Horse Channel on YouTube.

New resources are regularly updated on Kathleen's and my: **www.theSoulofaHorse.com** or our blog **http://thesoulofahorse.com/blog**

Liberated Horsemanship at:
http://www.liberatedhorsemanship.com/
Scroll down to the fifth Article in the column on the right entitled Barefoot Police Horses

An article about the Houston Mounted Patrol on our website: Houston Patrol Article

The following are links to videos on various subjects, all found on our The Soul of a Horse Channel on YouTube:

Video of Joe: Why Are Our Horses Barefoot?

Video of Joe: Why Our Horses Eat from the Ground

Video: Finding The Soul of a Horse

Video of Joe and Cash: Relationship First!

Video: The Soul of a Horse Paddock Paradise: What We Did, How We Did It, and Why

Don't Ask for Patience – God Will Give You a Horse

The next 2 links are to very short videos of a horse's hoof hitting the ground. One is a shod hoof, one is barefoot. Watch the vibrations roll up the leg from the shod hoof... then imagine that happening every time any shod hoof hits the ground: to view go to The Soul of a Horse Channel on YouTube:

Video: Shod Hoof
Video: Barefoot Hoof

Find a recommended trimmer in your area:

http://www.aanhcp.net

http://www.americanhoofassociation.org

http://www.pacifichoofcare.org

http://www.liberatedhorsemanship.com/

Valuable Links on Diet and Nutrition:

Dr. Juliette Getty's website:
http://gettyequinenutrition.biz/

Dr. Getty's favorite feed/forage testing facility:
Equi-Analytical Labs:
http://www.equi-analytical.com

For more about pretty much anything in this book
please visit one of these websites:

www.thesoulofahorse.com

http://thesoulofahorse.com/blog

www.14handspress.com

www.thesoulofahorseblogged.com

The Soul of a Horse Fan Page on Facebook

The Soul of a Horse Channel on YouTube

Joe and The Soul of a Horse on Twitter
@Joe_Camp

Made in the USA
Middletown, DE
26 August 2017